UNSHAKEABLE
CONFIDENCE
YOUR BLUEPRINT

UNSHAKEABLE CONFIDENCE YOUR BLUEPRINT

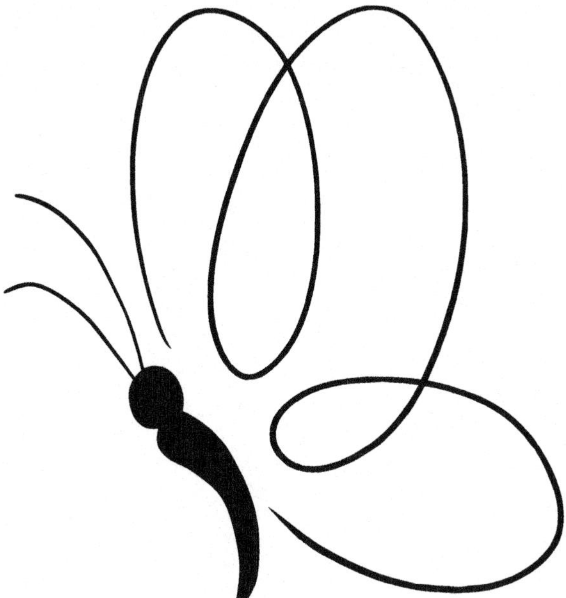

KIRSTEEN WILLIAMSON-GUINN

Unshakeable Confidence - Your Blueprint

ISBN: 978-1-0687655-0-6

Published by: Kirsteen Williamson-Guinn | Elevate Women
Editor: Lisa de Caux | LDC Editorial
Design and Production: Catherine Williams | Chapter One Book Design

Printed in the United Kingdom

PRAISE FOR *UNSHAKEABLE CONFIDENCE*

If you are wondering why you should pick up this brilliantly useful book, allow me to share my experience of working with Kirsteen and adopting her Unshakeable Confidence System.

As a graduate of Kirsteen's 12-week programme, I now possess the tools that enable me to flourish in a world that often expects women to juggle multiple roles and responsibilities.

Kirsteen came into my life at a crucial time when I had just been promoted and was grappling with imposter syndrome. Through her programme, accompanied by regular coaching sessions, she helped me uncover my power. I learned not only to believe in myself wholeheartedly but also to create a vision for my life and career with priorities, put myself first, and let go of guilt and behaviours that were getting in my way. It truly has been transformational.

I will continue to work with Kirsteen in the future because she has made such a huge difference in my life. This book is like having a confidence first aid kit in my pocket, ready to guide and support me whenever I need it. I wholeheartedly recommend this book to anyone seeking to unlock their potential and achieve the life they desire.

Louise Wilce

I cannot begin to express the profound impact that Kirsteen's programme has had on my life. During one of the darkest periods I have ever experienced, dealing with the intense pain of bereavement, her guidance and support were nothing short of a lifeline. Her programme provided me with the tools and strategies I needed to navigate my grief, helping me to process my emotions and find a path forward.

What sets her programme apart is the personalised attention and genuine care she offers. Kirsteen's support has been instrumental in rebuilding my confidence. With her encouragement, I was able to gradually regain my sense of self-worth and believe in my abilities once again. This newfound confidence empowered me to take bold steps towards creating a legacy that honours my dear late husband, Justin and reflects the person I have become.

Moreover, Kirsteen's programme did not just help me survive my grief; it enabled me to thrive beyond it. Through her coaching, I discovered a renewed passion for my career and, ultimately, landed my dream job. This achievement felt like a distant possibility during my darkest days, but her unwavering support made it a reality. Her programme has been a beacon of hope and transformation in my life, guiding me to a place of peace, purpose, and fulfillment.

I am immensely grateful for her wisdom, compassion, and dedication. The programme is not just about overcoming obstacles; it's about unlocking your potential and living a life filled with meaning and joy. For anyone facing challenges, I wholeheartedly recommend this programme—it truly has the power to change lives.

I still continue to work with Kirsteen, as her ongoing support and guidance remain invaluable to me. She is a continual source of strength and inspiration, helping me to grow and achieve even more.

Eilish Byrne-Whelehan

CONTENTS

PROLOGUE

Thank you!

Thank you for buying this book.

Thank you for investing in yourself.

Thank you for trusting me as your guide on this journey.

I want you to know something.

You have ALL the confidence you need.

You are more capable than you can begin to imagine.

You have more possibilities and potential than you will ever know.

In this book, I am going to help you to see and tap into that.

First, though, why would you listen to me?

Let me tell you a little bit about myself.

I spent thirty-two years in banking. I had a great career for the most part. Always confident and successful, on the outside!

A few years before I left my job and started building my business, I started to train as a health coach, because I knew I wanted to work for and on myself and do something useful for others.

I didn't know at that point that I would become my own first client.

Eighteen months before I left my career, my dad was diagnosed terminally ill and my mum's dementia started to take a grip of her.

This was a real turning point for me.

I suddenly felt totally out of control, like the roof was caving in. I was getting through the week on soya cappuccinos, wine, and whatever food I could eat on the run.

I felt stressed, sad, and helpless. I felt I had lost my confidence and myself.

I created a programme which got me through these tough times and realised that this was the work I wanted to do.

I wanted to offer an alternative to time off sick, or medication, which was basically what I was offered. So that's what I did.

Over the next couple of years, I learned so much from working with my amazing clients, but I also did more coaching certifications and studied all things confidence with a passion.

This has led me to where I am now: four years into running my own business.

Taking good care of myself, even when things are so difficult. After eight years of dementia, I lost my beautiful mum in March 2023.

My mum never really understood my job, or why I wasn't around much, but I am so glad that I was around for her, Covid allowing, for her last few years.

She taught me to pay attention to the little things and enjoy every moment of life. I know it's cheesy, but we really do only get one go at this.

My dad gave me my work ethic and drive, and my mum showed me how to appreciate what I have created.

My aim with this book is to provide you with a wealth of theory, exercises, stories, and case studies. My goal is to equip you with practical tools that you can apply in your life, rather than simply acquiring knowledge.

Ultimately, I hope to empower you to embody the unshakeably confident woman that is within you.

So, let's get going!

THINGS I WANT YOU TO KNOW ABOUT CONFIDENCE

There are two types of confidence – situational confidence and core confidence.

We all have situational confidence. For example, if someone asked me to get on stage and talk to people about confidence, I would love to do that. These situations are familiar to me, so I have the confidence to do it without too much concern.

However, if someone said to me "put those ice skates on and dance around the ice rink", I would not have situational confidence. Nope, not at all.

I would have to go deep into my core confidence and find all the things I can trust in myself so that I could even stand up in those skates.

Maybe you would be happier to put the ice skates on. We are all wired differently because of our experiences and beliefs.

What I have worked on myself, with my clients and now I want to work on with you, is building that core confidence.

The trust you can build in yourself to face any challenge confidently. You will start to learn, that you don't lose or lack confidence, you just become disconnected from yourself and all that you bring. Fully connecting back to yourself, allows you to tap into your brilliance and therefore feel more confident.

The other thing I want you to know is that confidence is built on your successes AND your failures.

Success is not a linear path; we learn and grow from our failures and setbacks even more than we do from our successes.

Take a second now and think about all the things that didn't go to plan in your life. The things that in that moment felt like failures. Now look at how you have grown from those experiences and start to look for the things that you can trust in yourself, even when things don't go to plan.

The third thing I want you to know is that we block our own confidence. I know! Why would we do that?

Imagine you are at work, and your boss says to you, "I would like you to present to your board/Exco tomorrow, share with them your work so far on the project you're leading."

You might, first of all, have a wobble. Then you forget all your brilliance, skills and gifts that have got you to here and you totally underestimate yourself. You go back to that doubting little girl inside, and you are disconnected from the mature fully-resourced version of you that you are today.

When you realise you are doing that, you give yourself a good talking-to and swing into overestimating yourself.

You tell yourself, "Of course, I can do this! I have totally got this." In that moment, we are blind to the things we need to support us to do this brilliantly. We might need to talk to someone on your board/Exco first and get the lay of the land. We might need to brush up on presentation skills. We might need to revisit the last Exco slide deck to understand what's on their minds.

When we swing from underestimating (not good enough) to overestimating (more than good enough) we block our confidence. We want to stand in our power, know what we are good at and work on the things that make us even better, if they are important to what we are doing.

Does this resonate?

I wonder if this will too.

The three most common things that drain our confidence...

External factors – this could be your friends, family, the news, or something else in your external world that drains your confidence. I am going to tell you something really obvious now. Sorry, not sorry! Do less of this stuff. If you know there are people in your life that drain your confidence, spend less time with them. I know it might be difficult, but it is so important that you choose consciously who you spend your time with.

The same with the news. It is depressing. Five months after quitting my corporate job and kissing goodbye to my lovely salary on the 23rd of every month, COVID-19 hit. We went into lockdown, the meetings with corporates I had booked into my diary were cancelled, all I saw on the news was fear and uncertainty, and I was thinking *what have I done?* The more I listened to the news, the more nervous I became.

This is not about being an ostrich and sticking your head in the sand. It is about consuming what is necessary and then creating your own agenda.

As Warren Buffet says, "The best protection against inflation is your own personal earning power" (tinyurl.com/own-earning-power). Interestingly lots of people became more reflective of what was really important to them during Covid, and I have learned that being in charge of my own income, business and life is the way I want to be. Even when it is difficult! At least I get to make my own choices.

The point is if you know things/people drain your confidence, restrict, or eliminate, the time you spend with them.

The next thing that can drain your confidence is your inner world. You know, that really annoying voice in your head. The one that tells you to stop imagining that you can do all this stuff and asks, "who do you think you are?" or "you are not smart enough to do that". "What makes you think people will listen to you?!" The same voice I had in my head at the start of writing this book.

You know this, the voice is yours. You can tell her to be quiet, give her a name, have a sarcastic funny conversation with her where you are in charge.

Turn up the volume of the voice in you that is confident and courageous.

I am not saying push away the annoying voice; I am saying turn the positivity volume up.

The annoying voice will have a positive intention for you. It wants to keep you safe, so hear what it has to say, thank it and consider if there is anything you need to take on board, and then get focused on who you are being. Who you are being, is a more powerful focus than what you are doing!

I find journaling really useful here. If there is something on your mind, something unhelpful, you can use this neat little model to work through your next steps.

Let me introduce you to **S.T.E.A.R.**

> **Situation** – The situation is always neutral (okay, apart from extreme things). Our day-to-day life for the majority of us is neutral.
>
> **Thoughts** – This is what determines how we feel about the situation. Whether it is good or bad.
>
> **Emotions/Feelings** – Our thoughts create our feelings, which then determine our ...
>
> **Action** – How do we respond if we are angry, upset, frustrated, versus happy, reflective, calm?

We want to give ourselves the best possible experience, so do your best not to act on unhelpful emotions. You are likely to knee jerk or have a poorer quality action if you do that.

> **Result** – Your outcome is not a result of your situation; it always starts from the thoughts you have. Remember you are totally in control of them. You can choose

to look at things from multiple perspectives. That in itself is a great way to diffuse a challenging situation.

Next time you feel stuck in a loop of unhelpful thoughts, grab your journal and use S.T.E.A.R. You will find it very useful, and it will help you move forward in a constructive way.

I know you are wondering: what's the third thing that drains our confidence?

Well, it is comparison, or compare and despair. You know that thing you do, when you look at someone else and think 'Oh my goodness, they are amazing', then immediately go to 'I would never be able to do that because of x and y.'

This is another one of those times when we disconnect from our own brilliance.

I have a couple of practical tips here that will help you stay connected to yourself and feel good in the presence of other people's brilliance.

Firstly, amplify whatever it was that you admired in that person by telling them. Did you know that studies show that when you lift one woman up, she will then lift ten more up as a consequence. Tell her what you love!

Hopefully you are feeling good now because you have made someone else feel good.

Secondly, think about the particular thing in that person that you admire. Is it important to you? Will it support you in your goals and aspirations? If not, then you are done. You have celebrated someone else's brilliance, she has then gone on to do the same, and you are good.

If it is something that is important to you and would support the fulfilment of your goals and aspirations, think about what you can learn from this person. How could you learn what they have done? What support do you need? Who could help you? What difference would this make to you?

You see, having this two-stage approach changes everything. You have moved beyond the comparison; you feel good because you have amplified someone else's brilliance. They now feel good and are doing the same for others, AND you are rationally assessing what, if anything, you can learn from this that will help you in the pursuit of your goals.

This will take practice, like many things, and we need to retrain our response.

With that in mind, before we move on, I encourage you to think about the last time you experienced compare and despair and walk yourself through this two-stage process.

Ready to move on?

We have covered some truths and myths about confidence, how we block our confidence and the three ways we drain our confidence.

You have heard my story and why I do what I do now.

I would like to acknowledge the Health Coach Institute (www.healthcoachinstitute.com) for getting me on my own health journey and helping me start to find my niche and build my business.

I would also like to acknowledge Claire Zammit and

Sara Wilson from Evolving Wisdom, Feminine Power (femininepower.com).

During my two-year journey with them, I have delved into my self-discovery, which has been transformational for me and empowered me to serve my clients in a deeper and more impactful manner.

All of my experiences and studies, have led me to create my Unshakeable Confidence System. It is designed to help you regain your **SPIRIT** and tap into your Unshakeable Confidence by focusing on key elements that work together harmoniously.

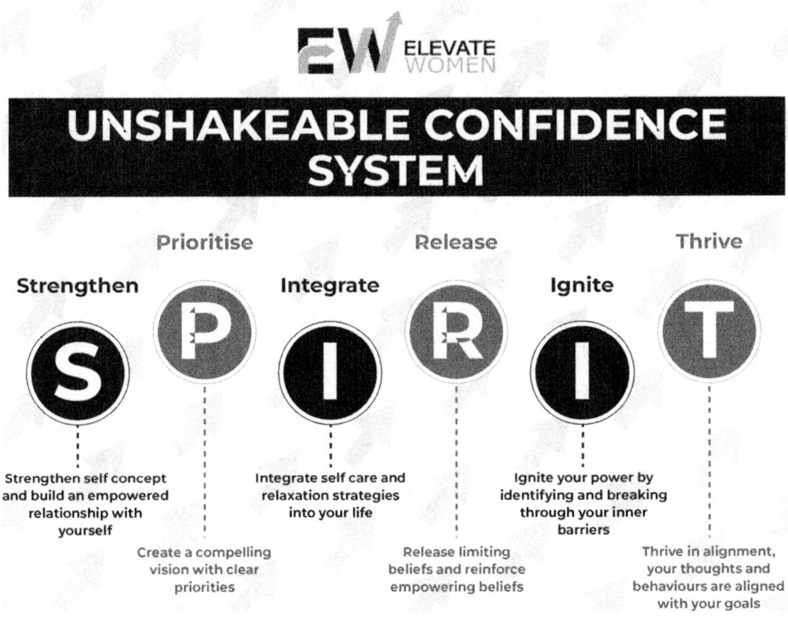

We start with **Strengthen** – strengthening your self-concept and relationship with yourself. Everything starts with you.

Next, we **Prioritise**, creating a compelling vision with clear priorities.

Then we **Integrate** self-care and relaxation techniques, calm is confident.

Then we **Release** those limiting beliefs that are holding you back, strengthening the foundation of your mindset.

Now we can **Ignite Your Power** by breaking through inner barriers and unlocking your true potential.

Finally, you are ready to **Thrive** by aligning your thoughts, habits, and behaviours with the boldest version of yourself.

Use this **SPIRIT** blueprint to identify and focus on the areas that need your attention, ensuring that each component is in balance and supporting your journey to Unshakeable Confidence.

We will work through each of these as we progress through the book, building on each element.

You might like to complete this quiz so you can see where to focus your efforts: https://kirsteen-kldndktp.scoreapp.com/p/main-landing-page

Now, before we dive into the blueprint, think about something you would like to create in your life.

Who would you be if you had unshakeable confidence?

What would you be doing, that you are not currently doing?

Make a note of your thoughts and ideas before you move on.

I really would like this book to be a journey of learning and implementation for you to create the outcomes you desire, rather than a book that you eventually read and then just think it was a good read! My intention is that this book is transformational for you, and for that to happen, you will need to participate in each chapter.

Are you up for that?

Really?

Pinky promise?

I trust you, so let's get started

You will find note pages at the end of each chapter.

CHAPTER 1

STRENGTHEN

SELF-CONCEPT AND RELATIONSHIP WITH SELF

Self-concept is the missing link that is often overlooked or not talked about. Your self-concept—how you perceive and understand yourself—shapes every aspect of your life. At the core of this is the relationship you have with yourself.

By prioritising self-care and building an empowered relationship with yourself you lay the foundation for a strong, positive self-concept. This isn't just about treating yourself well; it's about knowing yourself deeply, respecting your needs, and believing in your worth.

When you nurture this relationship, you build resilience, authenticity, and self-love, all of which reinforce a self-concept that is confident, grounded, and capable of guiding you through life's challenges with clarity and purpose.

It is time to invest in the relationship you have with yourself. Imagine if you didn't beat yourself up when things go wrong. Instead, you started showing yourself compassion and empathy.

Imagine if you nurtured and nourished yourself when you were trying to do something new, instead of expecting it to be done perfectly.

Imagine how much difference that would make in your life and how you feel.

The most important relationship we have is so often the poorest and least invested in – the relationship we have with ourselves.

Now is the time for us to change this, because when this changes other things change with much more ease and flow.

One of the most important ways we can invest in ourselves is by checking in and seeing how we are feeling and what we need. Not checking in with our head, but reconnecting with our body, being still and paying attention to what we are feeling.

When I was at my most stressed, I was too scared to even think about how I was feeling, let alone feel what I was feeling. I thought if I stopped for too long to think about it, I might fall over and not get back up!

We need to turn towards ourselves and face what we are feeling. Then we can do something to help ourselves feel better. This is how we become more resourceful for ourselves.

Remember I mentioned, that when we are disconnected from ourselves it can feel like we have lost our confidence. When we are connected to ourselves, we know everything we need is within ourselves. It is a matter of tuning in and paying attention.

This is where I start with my clients, and I encourage them to check in with themselves every day.

This is something that has really helped me. Being able to sit with my emotions instead of pushing them away or suppressing them is very healing. Even though at first it felt very scary. When you are being resourceful for your own needs you can be creative about the things you can do to support yourself and feel good.

There is a recording of how to check in with yourself each day as part of this book's Resources Section. I encourage you to build these two minutes into your daily routine.

Whatever it is you are looking to create, you need you on your best form. Talking to yourself nicely, cheering yourself on, and providing what you need for yourself.

I remember my business coach asking me to rate my performance. My performance! I was always really happy talking about my business; anything to do with it, I would be candid about. But asking me about my own performance created all sorts of emotions. It brought up a bit of shame, as I knew there were things that I needed to take care of, and guilt, because I knew I wasn't doing anything about it. Feelings of not being good enough, that old chestnut.

You need to fuel and nourish the vessel that is taking you to your destination. And there were definitely some gaps in my performance to that end.

Before I became certified as a health coach, I had tried every diet under the sun and not really lost weight. I was not a healthy vegan – too much coffee and wine and poor choices when I was in a rush, which was most of my time in my old corporate life.

Then I changed my relationship with food, learned that *how* we eat is as important as *what* we eat, and the weight came off. I started to nourish and nurture myself and invest in my relationship with me.

Then over the last three years, I have had lockdown, peri-menopause, and a busy diary, which means I have been sitting at this desk too much. Sitting apparently is the new smoking. I also realised that I wasn't owning my health and weight gain. As I write this now, I am getting a handle back on my health and starting to feel better. It is amazing what a bit more exercise can do, and I am making much healthier food choices and eating slowly again.

Taking care of ourselves doesn't have to be difficult. These are the things we need to pay attention to:

- The food we eat – Food that energises us and we feel good after we have eaten it
- Hydration – Easy on the caffeine and drink lots of water and herbal teas
- Stress Release – yoga/meditation

- Sleep – How many hours do you need to feel rested? Do you have a wind-down routine to ensure a good night's sleep?
- Social Connection – Love and friendships
- Movement – even twenty minutes walking a day makes a difference

As you look at this list, pick two things that you know would make a difference to your health if you did them. They can be two little things. It is always good to start small and build; that is how you transform.

You are the best authority on you. Your body tells you what it likes and what it doesn't, so pay attention and give yourself more of the good stuff.

Optimise your health by connecting back into your body and paying attention to what it is telling you – your body is an amazing vessel; pay attention, respect, and nurture it and you will find that other areas of your life improve too.

There are also a multitude of apps that help us to do this.

So, what do you want?

This is often the hardest question to answer. I have had many clients really struggle to answer this question, and so did I.

If we are trying to answer this from our head, we will struggle. This is one for us to connect to our intuition and really tune in to what we yearn for.

Once you have settled in and tuned in, here are four questions that might help and journalling on them will help even more.

What would you most like to create in your life?

What would you most like to contribute in your life?

What would you most like to express in your life?

What would you most like to experience in your life?

Let your pen/pencil be free and journal away on this. We don't need to start thinking ahead or trying to figure out how to do these things, we just need to connect to the things we yearn for.

You can find lots of meditations to help with this on the Insight Timer App.

Now you have some answers, pick one, the one that feels like it will lead to other great outcomes, and decide that is what you are directing your attention and energy towards throughout this book.

Who do you need to be to create this change in your life?

What is the most obvious next step towards this in total alignment with who you are becoming?

I know this might feel a bit weird. Let me share an example of mine.

When I was building my business at the beginning, I made decisions from a place of success and working with many clients. Even though that wasn't true, I would ask myself, what would the version of me that is in demand and successful do next towards this goal?

Who are you becoming and what's your next step?

We may make the mistake of thinking that we need to know all the steps before we can take the first step. That is what holds so many of us back and stops us from becoming who we are meant to be.

How can you champion yourself with this goal? I know you champion so many other people, it is time for you to champion yourself. What does that look like for you?

Throughout this book there are going to be mindset shifts I ask you to play with.

The most important shift for this chapter is the shift from perfection to progress.

As a self-confessed recovering perfectionist, I know how damaging striving for perfection can be.

This can be another reason not to do something, or we beat ourselves up because we didn't do it perfectly.

Nope, no, that's not how we operate anymore.

Perfection is the lowest standard you can have for yourself because it is unobtainable. Just sit with that for a moment.

I am here for progress. Celebrate every tiny bit of progress you make. It feels good, it builds momentum, you can get where you want to be and feel good.

When we feel good, good things happen, this has been true for me and my clients and is something I always come back to as and when I fall out of alignment with my vision.

SUMMARY POINTS FOR CHAPTER 1

- The relationship we have with ourselves is THE most important relationship we have. Make time for it, become your own best friend.
- What two things can you do to improve your self-care that you know will make you feel better?
- Get out of your head, get into your body and start to create some clarity about the things you would like to create, experience, contribute and express in your life.
- Let yourself feel. Turn towards your feelings instead of suppressing them or pushing them away.
- Mindset shift, from perfection to progress

RESOURCES

- Daily Check-in

See page 100 for links to all the Resources

SPACE FOR YOUR OWN THOUGHTS

SPACE FOR YOUR OWN THOUGHTS

SPACE FOR YOUR OWN THOUGHTS

SPACE FOR YOUR OWN THOUGHTS

P

CHAPTER 2

PRIORITISE

CREATE A COMPELLING VISION WITH CLEAR PRIORITIES

Now you are strengthening the relationship you have with yourself, it's time to prioritise the things that are important to you.

Clarity is a brilliant confidence builder. Being clear about your priorities and confident that they are all taken care of is what we are aiming for here.

This analogy helped me to look at things differently.

Life is like my weeknight cooking...

Sometimes I throw everything into the pan and hope for the best.

Many of my clients want to feel happy, calm, and confident. When we first start working together, they feel anxious, out of control and like they are holding back.

It is so easy to feel out of control if we are throwing everything into our week and hoping for the best.

Instead of treating our life like a weeknight dinner and throwing whatever is lurking at the back of our fridge into our pot, we need to treat our life like a beautiful fairy cake.

We consciously choose the quality and quantity of ingredients that make our cake.

Cooking and baking need different processes. So do living and thriving!

Consciously choosing how we feel, how we spend our time and what we are focused on can change our experience and our results.

What's the one thing you can choose today that will help you thrive?

I am going to start with the mindset shift needed for this chapter and this stage in your journey of creating your chosen life, that beautiful fairy cake.

The shift from **reaction** to **creation**. Shifting from "reaction" to "creation" (my favourite shift) means I shift my focus from reacting to what is going on around me, to me being in the driving seat of my life. Bringing all my resources and skills to respond to creating the life I desire. Instead of giving my time to other people's priorities, I am making time for my own priorities.

What I love about this is that both words, reaction and creation, have the same letters, they are ordered differently. That is what we need to do with our life sometimes – order it differently.

Let me explain.

I spent the ten years before I left my career reacting to other people's goals. I made money for the company I worked for and implemented their plans.

I didn't stop to wonder what I really wanted.

I didn't stop.

Have you stopped to answer that question?

I know this is the toughest question to answer, but if you don't know what you want, then you won't have clear priorities that take you to your goal and you won't then be intentional with your time.

Your time could well be taken, like mine was, by other people's stuff.

Then, by the time I had done that, I would not have time left for me – I would then be in scarcity mode.

"I don't have enough time for myself to do the things I want to do".

Is this a story you are familiar with?

The truth is THE most successful people have the same number of hours as we have in the day. I know that is a cliché, but this is something I remind myself of all the time.

It helps me be intentional with my time.

First things first – what are your top five priorities in life?

Mine are:

1. My health (mental and physical) – yes, that comes first because, when I don't prioritise it, I am not on full power
2. My relationships
3. My business
4. Fun
5. My contribution

In case you need some help to clarify your priorities, you can use the *Wheel of Life* (as shown in the Resources Section) to assess how happy you are with the key areas of life and that will help you determine where your time and focus are needed.

When you are scoring how happy you are in each area, remember that some areas will be more important to you than others. Which are the most important and which would have the biggest impact on your life if you were to work on them?

What are your priorities? If business or career are in your top five priorities, you may want to break those down into a further five priorities, so you can ensure you are spending your time on the right things.

For most of us, business or career are the biggest use of our time, so, again, we need to make sure we are clear about the outcomes we are looking to create in our business/career.

I will give you an example of something that didn't work for me.

One of my growth edges (room for improvement, development, or expansion), and something that is make or break for my business, is sales and marketing. The issue is I never really wanted to spend my time on sales or marketing, so guess what, I did everything else before I did that.

Funny thing: without sales or marketing, I am reliant on my clients coming to me. Now sometimes that happens, but most of the time it doesn't. Not without me doing some sales or marketing first.

What was I doing? All the other stuff first. The stuff that I can do, that is easier, but that isn't really a needle mover in my business.

In my personal life, for a long time, I didn't prioritise my health. I didn't sleep well or have the energy I wanted. I didn't feel like doing much at the weekends, and, during the week, I was running on empty.

Can you see what I mean about being intentional?

Please, for me, look at your list of priorities and now look at your calendar and check: how much time do you have allocated to your priorities? I never used to schedule fun! What are you not scheduling? Then look at the things that are not a priority and remove them. Yes, you can do it. If they are not a priority, why are they taking your time?

I know. It can feel really difficult to take things out of our diaries when we have already accepted them. That's why it is so important that we don't accept calendar invites if they are not in alignment with our priorities.

If you have a VA/PA who manages your diary, they will need your support and clear communication to make sure this happens for you.

I want you to absorb this into your being.

If you don't value your time, how can you expect others to?

Saying yes to everything will lead to stress, burnout and the unfulfillment of you and your priorities.

When you say yes to everything, you will either end up having to say no to something more important, or you will have to work silly hours to get everything done.

This doesn't mean you have to say no and be unhelpful.

This just means you have to be really helpful and ensure the right things happen in the right way and by the right person.

Instead of saying an immediate yes, try this: **"Let me get back to you"**.

Give yourself time to consider if what you are being asked is in alignment with your priorities.

If not, then:

- Suggest someone who can do it instead
- Say it is not one of your priorities, so is there someone else who can do this?

If your boss is asking you to do this, say it isn't one of your priorities, so if you do it, you will have to drop something else or do it in an extended timescale.

(Always useful to get your boss to agree with your priorities ahead of these types of conversations. It makes things much easier for both parties.)

The really important thing is to shift out of a reaction of saying yes to everything and being more considered and transparent about what you spend your time on.

How often do you prioritise someone or something else over your health (mental and/or physical) or the fun stuff you like to do?

If you don't schedule these activities, you will continue to do that.

The things you do for yourself are more important than anything else in your diary. So please start putting you in there and treating time set aside for you as your most important meeting. I promise you will thank me for this.

Then you can look at your diary for the week ahead at the start of every week and look at how much time you have allocated for your priorities. Does everything have the amount of time necessary? Are there things that shouldn't be taking your time? Are there things that should be in there but aren't? You can take care of this because you are focused on it and if you are out of your "serial yes habit", there is likely to be less repair work to be done at the start of your week.

There is something else really important to factor into your priorities, and that is time to grow and develop in any ways necessary to achieve/create what you are working on.

- You might need to learn something new, complete a training course, or attend classes
- You might need to hire a coach and gain the support you need as you step outside of your comfort zone
- You might need to read certain books or attend meetings
- You might need to join a new network or mix in a different circle

All of this takes time, and it is important you allocate time for this, because, in my experience, when we feel busy, or even overwhelmed, the first things we drop are those things that feel more difficult or are new. We stick with our familiar activities, even if we don't like them, or they are not important.

How many times have you done something mundane or that you disliked, so you can avoid doing something important?

Me too, that's life, that's why I always have a coach to keep me true to my plan.

To help you start to think about your growth plan there is a link to a template you can download in the Resources Section.

Part of your review for the week ahead should include prioritising your growth activities so you can achieve what's important to you!

SUMMARY POINTS FOR CHAPTER 2

- Mindset shift: from reaction to creation.
- Saying no to something means you can say yes to the important stuff.
- Get clear on YOUR priorities and schedule them.
- Shift from an automatic yes to considering how requests align with your priorities.
- Schedule time for yourself first and treat it as THE most important appointment you have.

RESOURCES

- Growth plan template
- Wheel of life

See page 100 for links to all the Resources

SPACE FOR YOUR OWN THOUGHTS

SPACE FOR YOUR OWN THOUGHTS

SPACE FOR YOUR OWN THOUGHTS

SPACE FOR YOUR OWN THOUGHTS

CHAPTER 3

INTEGRATE

SELF-CARE AND RELAXATION STRATEGIES

What has being relaxed got to do with confidence and achieving the things we want in our lives?

You remember the saying "cool as a cucumber".

This is the best way to be for our health, for eating, for thinking, for speaking, for being, for getting things done, for confidence, for everything.

I used to pride myself on being busy. The problem with that was I never had time to think, and when I did stop, I was so stressed, I didn't even know I had stopped.

That is true for many of us. Sadly, many of us are so disconnected from our body, we don't even know that we are often in a stressed state. I definitely denied being stressed. I just kept going and it became my natural state for a while.

Slowing down, and even stopping, allows you to gather yourself before meetings. I have clients who, years after working with me, still go to the toilet before a meeting and do their conscious breathing, just like I do.

In this chapter, we are going to shine a light on stress, what it does to us, and I will share my favourite ways to get your body out of a stressed state!

Firstly, stress is the opposite of relaxation. When do we feel stressed? Mostly when we are moving too fast. Stress can also occur because we are either focused on the past or worrying about what might happen in the future. Replaying something from our past that didn't go well can create recurring or prolonged feelings of stress. As can worrying about the future.

What we want to do, instead, is be present. When we are present, our relationships improve, our thinking is clearer, and we feel calmer. This is where we want to be.

Being present means maintaining a moment-by-moment awareness of our thoughts, feelings, bodily sensations, and surrounding environment.

An easy way to get yourself into the present is to ask yourself, what can I see? What can I feel? What can I taste? What can I smell? What can I hear? Engaging your senses and answering those questions can quickly take you out of a stressed state.

You may have heard of a hormone called cortisol? This is the hormone that is released when we are stressed out. Cortisol is an important and helpful part of the body's response to stress; however, it is important that the body's relaxation response is activated to return the body's functions to normal after a stressful event. Unfortunately, in the current high-stress culture, the body doesn't always have a chance to return to normal.

Higher and more prolonged levels of cortisol in the bloodstream have been shown to have negative effects, such as:

- Impaired cognitive performance
- Blood sugar imbalances
- Decreased bone density
- Higher blood pressure
- Lowered immunity
- Increased abdominal fat, which is associated with many serious health problems.

It is time to help our body return to a normal state quicker and spend more time in a relaxed state.

The number one way to stop producing so much cortisol is to slow down. Not easy I know. We are going to practice something that will help you slow down and can de-stress your body in two minutes.

This is called the 5–5–7 breath. You will inhale for 5, hold for 5 and exhale for 7 seconds.

Let's try it!

Sit in a comfortable position, spine straight and feet flat on the floor. Eyes can be open or closed. Inhale for 1, 2, 3, 4, 5, filling your lungs to two thirds' capacity. Hold for 5, 4, 3, 2, 1 and exhale for 7, 6, 5, 4, 3, 2, 1. As you continue this conscious breathing, scan your senses. The scent of the air in your nose, the red and oranges of your eyelids (if they are closed!), your taste buds. The feeling of your seat on the chair and your feet spread wide on the earth. Inhale, hold and exhale. Keep breathing and scanning, tuning into a heightened awareness and repeat this ten times.

This is two mins to inner calm, and you can do it anywhere, any time and it is free.

Even when there is chaos going on around you, pay attention to who you are being. Are you being someone who is busy and stressed, or someone who is slowing down and calm?

Practise using conscious breathing throughout the day and working in the rhythm of relaxation. You will find that you are more focused, more productive, and more energised.

We know there can be many stressors in our lives. Now you have two ways to increase the time and quality of your inner calm: conscious breathing and being present.

Let me introduce you to a client of mine. I started working with her last year; let's call her Suzy.

She came to me because she was struggling with anxiety and couldn't seem to focus.

Her personal issues were starting to take over her life and impact her work.

Over the first three weeks, we worked on conscious breathing and EFT (tapping) to reduce and manage her anxiety. We created a powerful visualisation exercise and a sleep routine, as she hadn't slept properly for ages.

I checked in with her at the beginning of the fourth week and since our third session she had slept better, and she's having more good days than bad.

It doesn't sound like much, does it? But I know how different that can make you feel, and, for her, it is a massive deal.

There is no point trying to achieve anything else when you are so stressed and anxious and not sleeping.

From that platform, Suzy could go on and achieve the things she really wanted in her life.

Sometimes, we can prioritise our careers over our health. Without our health we have nothing, so take good care of yourself first and you will be able to perform beyond your expectations in all aspects of your life.

Another tool I regularly use if I start to feel stressed is journalling. I find that the more I can get out of my head, the less stressed I feel. We are also far more rational when we write than when we think. Often, if we are stressed, our thinking can be a negative loop, where things become bigger and bigger and then we feel overloaded and overwhelmed.

People often say they want to journal, but they don't know what to write. I will include some journalling prompts in the resources.

Another important focus area for creating inner calm is getting good quality and enough sleep.

Sleeping is essential for our health and it is really difficult to sleep if you are not relaxed. Especially when you live most of your life in your head.

When I was at my most stressed, I would get to sleep really quickly, mostly because I was so exhausted. Running on empty is pretty exhausting. Then I would wake up at about 2.30 a.m. EVERY morning and struggle to get back to sleep.

I would have so many things going on in my mind: worrying about my mum, grieving for my dad, thinking about work, beating myself up for not saying something I wanted to say, and giving myself a hard time for not thinking something through properly or showing my frustrations. You know what I mean.

One of the best ways for me to get back to sleep was my Insight timer app. (insighttimer.com – other apps are available.) I absolutely love this app. No, I don't get any kickbacks for promoting it; I wish I did because I recommend it to all my clients. Because I love it so much, let me tell you why.

The free version has everything I need. I can choose my meditations based on the amount of time I have and what I most need at the time. I would always choose a twenty-minute sleep meditation and more often than not, by the time it was finished I was back asleep. Before I got into this habit, I would be lying awake until about 4.30 a.m. with my alarm going off at 5 a.m. I can't think of anything more frustrating and exhausting than this.

Now, disclaimer needed here. I do not profess to be "good" at meditating. I also have lots of clients who say to me, they are not "good" at meditating. Like me, because they were not meeting their own high expectations at something new, they stopped doing it. Then I realised, you don't need to be good at meditating, you just need to do it. Meditation stops me in my tracks and helps me to focus on my breathing. Both of these are invaluable.

Aside from meditation to go to sleep, I would encourage everyone to take even ten minutes at the start of their day to sit and breathe, with or without listening to a meditation app. How do you think setting your day up in this way could support you? For me, it sets the tone for my day. Calm and focused.

Back to sleep. I know plenty of people who struggle to get off to sleep at night, as well as those who wake up in the middle of the night and can't get back to sleep. That is why having a sleep routine in the evening is so helpful. Most of us have some sort of morning routine, but how many of us have a sleep routine?

Sleep is so important for our health and wellbeing. It helps with concentration, our general mood and reducing stress.

A good night's sleep is just as important as having a healthy diet and exercising.

Sleep is involved in the healing and repair of our heart and blood vessels. A continued lack of sleep can be associated with an increased risk of heart disease, kidney disease, high blood pressure, diabetes, dementia and stroke. Poor sleep is also linked to weight gain. Studies show that sleep-deprived people tend to consume more calories.

Sleep is important for good brain functionality. I know that if I am tired, I will struggle to concentrate. Good sleep can improve problem-solving skills and enhance memory.

Poor sleep habits are linked to adverse effects on blood sugar and can reduce insulin sensitivity. Mental health issues, such as depression, are also linked to poor-quality sleep.

With all of this in mind, it is time to make sure we all get our beauty sleep! As well as these worrying health consequences of poor sleep, lack of sleep will play havoc with our confidence levels.

Most adults need between seven and nine hours of sleep every night to function at their best.

Enough said?! Time to create a sleep routine or evening wind down. After all, just because you might be physically ready for bed, you need to let your brain know that. We can't just expect it to stop working when we turn the light off, especially given the amount of stimulation we give it, often before we go to sleep!

Here are my tips to ensure you get a good night's sleep:

- Practice the regular rhythms of sleep – go to bed and wake up at the same time each day
- Avoid having a TV in the bedroom
- Have serene and restful colours in your bedroom that encourage sleep

- Create total darkness and quiet, consider eye-shades/masks and earplugs
- Avoid caffeine or reduce it in the afternoon – it may inhibit sleep
- Avoid alcohol – it helps you get to sleep but makes your sleep interrupted and of poor quality
- Eat no later than two hours before bed
- Write your worries down. During your **Evening Wind Down**, write down things that are causing you anxiety and make plans for the next day to reduce your worry. It will free up your mind and energy to move into deep and restful sleep
- Take a hot salt or an aromatherapy bath. Raising your body temperature before bed helps to induce sleep
- Warm your middle with a hot water bottle, it will raise your core temperature and trigger the proper chemistry for sleep
- Play some relaxing music or meditate to help you get to sleep

Which of these are you going to add to your bedtime routine?

Whatever you are trying to create, it is so important that you are not trying to do this from a place of stress or pushing, where everything feels like a battle sometimes.

As one of life's "pushers", these are some of the shifts I made that helped me to stop pushing and align myself with the life I want, where things feel much easier.

Life is full of little shifts.

It is the little shifts that make the difference.

Shifting from "got to" to "get to" brings positive energy to the day ahead. When you add up all your "got to's", it isn't surprising that we start to feel stressed about what's on our plate.

Shifting from judgement to curiosity, opens up possibility rather than keeping us stuck in judgement about something. We can be very judgemental of ourselves, and when we are in that judgement loop that can create stress. Curiosity can quickly take you into repair, progress or solution mode, all of which are better than judgement and the stress that creates.

These and so many more are little shifts I have learned to make, and I work with clients so they can make those shifts too.

SUMMARY POINTS FOR CHAPTER 3

- Stress is terrible for our mind and body.
- If we don't tune in to our bodies, we won't even know if we are stressed; for many of us it is our emotional home.
- Calm is confident.
- Sleep is vital for our physical and mental health.
- Mindset shift: judgement to curiosity.

RESOURCES

- Journalling prompts
- Insight Timer app

See page 100 for links to all the Resources

SPACE FOR YOUR OWN THOUGHTS

SPACE FOR YOUR OWN THOUGHTS

SPACE FOR YOUR OWN THOUGHTS

SPACE FOR YOUR OWN THOUGHTS

CHAPTER 4

RELEASE

RELEASE LIMITING BELIEFS

What are beliefs?

Repeated thoughts become your beliefs. They influence the actions you take and eventually become how you see yourself.

It's a chain reaction: your thoughts lead to your feelings, which lead to your actions, which lead to your results. After proving yourself right over and over again, your thoughts become beliefs. Beliefs then become automatic thoughts that drive your behaviours. In other words, habits.

Beliefs are different from facts

- Facts are truths
- Beliefs can become more powerful than facts
- Beliefs can have a long-term impact on your life
- Beliefs are your attitude towards things; they create mental filters.

The two most common types of beliefs are:

1. Empowering
2. Disempowering

Limiting or disempowering beliefs take away the possibility of the possibility.

The best approach is to magnify and reinforce your empowering beliefs and minimise disempowering ones.

One of the most common beliefs I work with is the idea that we are not good enough, or not enough in some way. These beliefs are often formed at a very early age, and we carry them forward through life, even reinforcing them.

I want you to know, that whatever you believe about yourself, there will be many more of you, very successful talented women, who have very similar beliefs about themselves.

Being conscious of our beliefs and, if necessary, challenging them, is even more important for us women because studies show that women and girls are significantly more likely to make shame-based meaning in the event of setbacks and failures. We create a fixed meaning about ourselves. Have a think now about where you might be doing this. This client story may prompt some thoughts for you.

I started working with a client, who was working for an organisation that was restructuring. She had had a great career with them for many years, but she could see that her opportunities for growth were shrinking and the likelihood of her role falling away was increasing.

She knew she needed to step into the external market and start to connect with recruiters and other businesses to secure a role for herself. Obvious, right?

She had this idea and belief that if she started applying for roles externally, she would be disloyal to the company that had looked after her for years. She made this mean that she was disloyal and therefore this would be bad, she would be bad.

She was stuck doing nothing even though logic told her she needed to do something.

We had to start to challenge that belief and get her to start connecting with key people internally and externally, so she could see what and where the opportunities were.

All it took was for her to start to see clearly what was happening and how that was stopping her from getting where she wanted to get to. Then we could start to challenge and disrupt that behaviour. She began expanding her external network and enhancing her profile. Within just a few months, she was being invited to discuss new career opportunities.

As I mentioned, our beliefs inform our actions, so if we are carrying a belief that is unhelpful, like my client on this occasion, we are in a fixed mindset and therefore stuck where we are.

When it comes to your goal, what are your beliefs? Do they need to be challenged?

I remember when I was applying for one of my first senior positions, I received lots of (unrequested) support. By the time I went to the assessment, I had so many voices in my head, I totally lost who I was. I was busy trying to take on board all these other people's instructions and ideas. Needless to say, it didn't go well, and I didn't get the job.

I was really embarrassed because everyone thought I would easily get the job, and I didn't. I made it mean that I was terrible at assessments, and it stopped me from going for another job for a while. I was in a fixed mindset that I was terrible at assessments, so I disconnected from any growth opportunities, and I stayed stuck.

It took me some time to figure out that what I actually needed was a different approach. To be supported by one person, who I trusted, who was ahead of where I wanted to be. When I found them and accessed the right support, I performed much better in my assessment and was offered the role. True story! No difference in my skills or experience, just a different approach and mindset.

Something else that can keep us stuck – feeling like an imposter.

One of the main drivers of feeling like an imposter is the expectations we set for ourselves, particularly our need to be perfect.

The need to be perfect:

- Slows us down
- Holds us back
- Creates self-doubt and self-criticism
- And is unhealthy

I think we all accept that being perfect is also out of reach.

My invitation to you is, firstly, to adopt a mindset embracing the fact that your imperfections are what make you unique.

Secondly, to get comfortable taking imperfect action.

These two things will keep you moving forward and help you feel good about your progress and growth.

When I work with my clients I work on their beliefs and also their identity. How they see themselves and their potential is crucial.

Have you ever wondered why, despite having compelling goals to strive for, you find yourself frustrated with your inability to achieve them, or falling back into bad habits?

Self-sabotage, feeling like an imposter, backsliding, procrastination and self-doubt can all be connected back to our self-concept.

This is why self-concept is so important.

Self-concept is formed by:

- How we see ourselves
- What we see as possible for ourselves
- Our self-esteem – which is often formed by how others see us and the feedback we have received

There are many studies that show that women radically underestimate themselves, and men also underestimate women.

Women in particular find it more difficult to articulate their brilliance.

On top of that:

- Sometimes, the people that give us feedback, don't spend enough time thinking through the value of what they are giving us
- Sometimes we then receive it and take it to be true and important, even though it could be poor quality

And then we hold onto it – for a long, long time.

What makes us accept as true poor quality, unthought through feedback?

If we accept it we might start to see ourselves that way.

If you want extraordinary results, you must work on your self-concept.

For many of us women our self-concept doesn't match our potential and what's possible for ourselves.

Our self-concept shapes our experience; it is who we are. It determines what we believe about ourselves, what we expect for ourselves and what we can tolerate to receive. This becomes our "inner glass ceiling".

Traditional coaching will not work in this case, as it doesn't address the inner barriers at a self-concept level.

I have included a self-concept self-assessment in the Resources Section so you can see where you might need some focus.

Until my personal coaching and training over the last three years, I had no idea about my own inner glass ceiling.

The upper limits I had set for myself.

The expectations I had for myself.

In my experience now, I know that the inner glass ceiling is the biggest threat to our success, to our ability to achieve all the things we are capable of achieving.

If you are struggling in a particular area of your life, take a moment and consider the expectations you have for yourself in this area.

What are you prepared to tolerate and not tolerate?

Compare this to an area of your life that you seem to excel in or where it feels like you are in flow.

What is the difference in your expectations in these areas?

When your upper limit or inner glass ceiling is lower than your potential, this is where you might experience self-sabotage or undermining patterns. This happens because you act in ways that keep you within the confines of your self-imposed limits, preventing you from reaching your full potential.

Take a moment and reflect on this, it could be the most powerful ten minutes of your day and more.

SUMMARY POINTS FOR CHAPTER 4

- Beliefs can be more powerful than facts, yet they are just our thoughts on repeat.
- Our beliefs and identity shape what we expect and accept for ourselves, therefore we must pay attention to these and challenge disempowering beliefs and where we underestimate ourselves.
- The biggest block to our potential is our own inner glass ceiling.
- Mindset shift: from a fixed mindset to a growth mindset.

RESOURCES

- Self-Concept Self-Assessment

See page 100 for links to all the Resources

SPACE FOR YOUR OWN THOUGHTS

SPACE FOR YOUR OWN THOUGHTS

SPACE FOR YOUR OWN THOUGHTS

SPACE FOR YOUR OWN THOUGHTS

CHAPTER 5

IGNITE

IGNITE YOUR POWER

I have already mentioned our own inner glass ceiling and how we may block ourselves. So how do we ignite our power?

This is one of my favourite sessions with clients as it really is a game changer once you start to understand what has been going on and how we block ourselves.

Studies [tinyurl.com/TripartiteRelatedness] with thousands of successful women show that there are three main ways that we block our power. They are:

1. Repeating old patterns, habits and stories that hold us back and create "shame"
2. Disconnection from our own selves, our intuition as well as disconnection from a higher power, whether that is your higher self, the universe, God, or whatever you believe in. This disconnection creates feelings of "lack"

3. Isolation – the idea that we "should" be able to do everything ourselves, the idea of asking for help could mean we are seen as weak in the eyes of others

How do we deal with these three things?

Firstly, we pay close attention to our patterns. We all have patterns in the ways we behave that either help or hinder our progress. When we look closely at them and understand them better, we can disrupt the patterns that hinder us.

Behind every pattern, there is a story we tell ourselves; our behaviour creates the evidence to back up our story. Again, this can be helpful, or it can hinder us.

When we believe we are not good enough, one of the common patterns is over-giving, being more focused on others than we are on ourselves. Wanting to please others so we can feel that we are good enough, but, of course, we could burn out because we are not focused on our own needs, or we deprioritise them in favour of someone else's. When we burn out, we are not at our best, and therefore, it must be true, that we are not good enough.

That is one example. What do you see in your patterns?

For a moment, think about this thing that you are looking to achieve or create in your life. What happens that gets you stuck? What do you actually see yourself doing or not doing in this moment? In this moment, what is it that you are believing about yourself?

Once we can see it, we can challenge it, and that is the first thing we need to do when it comes to our patterns. There is no need for shame. Instead, we need to show ourselves empathy and compassion, for keeping going in spite of everything.

The antidote to shame is empathy.

Something we rarely show ourselves!

I worked with a client who was unhappy in her job. There was a restructure coming and, because she didn't feel heard, she didn't have confidence that the decisions being made about her would be good for her. Yet she wasn't speaking up and positioning herself, her wants and needs, to the organisation.

I see this a lot. I also see people wanting to be seen, yet hiding in some way. Then they feel overlooked.

With my client, we got to work on her self-concept, how she sees herself, how she speaks to herself and the things she sees as possible for herself. Once she tuned into herself and what was going on, she started to talk to herself in a more empowering way. She slowed down to really tune in to what she wanted. Within six weeks of working together, she was having more honest and challenging conversations with her boss. She also applied for a bigger role externally and after a five-stage interview process she was offered a role with a significant pay increase.

When you change how you feel about yourself, tune into the things you are doing which hold you back and start disrupting those patterns, everything changes!

This sounds simple, but my client had many uncomfortable moments with me. Now she can see the value in facing into the things she had been turning away from and trying to ignore for so long.

When it comes to disconnection, this is something I see all the time. It was a big problem for me. I was going so fast I didn't want to stop. I didn't give myself time to think or feel. They both terrified me! I kept going, being busy, focused on other things, disconnected from myself, who I am and what I bring. Never having enough or being enough.

Learning how to reconnect has been a game changer for me and it often is for my clients.

We often disconnect from our adult fully resourced self in times of challenge. In those moments it is common to revert to our younger self, and feel those feelings of insecurity, panic and stress that we may have felt as a child. We disconnect from our qualities that we need to get us through the challenge we are facing.

In those moments, it is crucial to slow down, breathe and reconnect with who we really are and everything we bring. Follow the check-in audio exercise shown in Chapter 1. When you know what you are feeling and what you need, you can more often than not provide it for yourself.

As I look back on how I was a few years ago, I was like a pressure cooker. Keeping a lid on everything but knowing that the lid was going to come off at some point and make a mess everywhere! That's why I kept a lid on it. No one knew what was going on for me, because, like so many, I became an expert at hiding my true self and portraying someone who had it all together.

Then I learned how to face into my feelings and journal and get things out of my head instead of holding onto everything, trying to keep it together. Many of us spend most of our time in our heads. The challenge there is most of what goes on in our heads is repetitive and predictable, and a big chunk of our brain is designed to keep us safe, so when we are doing anything new, it will be interpreted as scary. Then that part of our brain will tell us to avoid it.

That's where being connected to your body and especially your intuition or gut wisdom is so helpful. For years we have been taught to override our intuition and pay attention to other people, the so-called experts. Our intuition is fully developed. Our ability to pay attention to it isn't. That's where the work is needed.

If I had £1 for every time one of my team or another colleague asked me what the next step in their career should be, I would be a millionaire. Really. What do I know about what is best for someone else? We are taught to look outward, rather than inward. We are taught to trust people more senior than us, people in certain positions.

The problem is unless they take the time to find out all about us, what we love, don't love, what makes us tick, what we are good at and so much more, they will give us bad or really obvious advice. The sad thing is many of us will receive this, much like bad feedback, and believe it to be true, overriding our own gut feelings and knowledge.

Sometimes it is harder to tune into our body because we have stuck energy stored there. It could be feelings of anger, anxiety, or frustration. When you have this stuck energy, it might feel like you are not bringing all of you to your life; there is a part of you that is blocked off.

We need to be able to release this stuck energy to help us truly unlock our power. You can do this through meditation, yoga, screaming into a pillow, exercise AND there is something else that is essential to releasing this stuck energy.

This is often the part that my clients resist the most.

This analogy often helps. Imagine you are looking in your kitchen cupboards. What are the chances of you finding a jar of something best before 2019? It is guaranteed in my kitchen cupboards. I am not a domestic goddess, and I am good with that.

I always find something out of date, and toxic, knocking about at the back of my cupboards. Taking up space, no longer relevant and certainly not useful.

That's what happens with our mind and body if we don't spring clean often.

Forgiveness is the way we spring clean. I invite you now to grab some paper that you can throw away (if you prefer) afterwards. Sit privately, nice, and relaxed, and write down everyone and everything you need to forgive or need to release. As things come into your head, just jot them down, what/who and why you are forgiving.

Remember to include yourself in this exercise. I have done this many times over and there are so many things I needed to forgive myself for.

The other thing to remember is forgiveness doesn't mean you condone the other person's behaviour.

Forgiving someone is about you. It puts you back in control; it is liberating you from feeling a victim.

So, let's get going now, and when you feel like you have forgiven everyone and everything, write another page. You can then choose what to do with your notes. Burn, bury, shred, whatever feels good.

When you do this, it can feel tough, but afterwards you will feel much lighter. Like you have released some things you have been holding onto unnecessarily.

This is not a 'once and done' though. It is something to do regularly, along with the meditation, breathing and yoga. You will know when you start to feel that stuck energy come back and you now know how to take care of yourself.

I want you to remember – when it comes to you and your life, you are the expert!

When you are looking to do something new, you are likely to come across many "so-called experts". It is easy to pay attention to them and override your own thoughts, feelings, and ideas. Check their credentials. What makes them an expert? If they are not an expert, just a well-intended person with an opinion, trust your gut and find someone a few steps ahead of you.

If, like me, you have spent years being in your head and have struggled to pay attention to your gut, then this will take practice, but I assure you it is worth it. As I mentioned in Chapter 1, I would encourage you to check in with yourself every day.

It is also important to remember that we are all part of something bigger. Whatever we believe in, it can help to remember that and home in on where our faith is.

A question for you. How often do you resist asking for or receiving support?

For some weird reason, many of us believe that we "should" be able to do everything ourselves.

Even the things that we have never done before and have had no training or learning experience of.

When you think about it, it's quite wild!

Think about the thing you are looking to create in your life. The purpose for you reading this book.

Now ask yourself:

What or who could support me to achieve this quicker, easier and with less mistakes or barriers?

Who has already done what you are looking to do?

Smart people learn from those who are slightly further ahead of them.

They have walked the path. They know how to get there, and they will help you avoid the mistakes they made.

In writing this book, I have hired people to help me. As an entrepreneur I have got used to hiring other people. I know what I am good at and spend my time doing as much of that as possible. As best as I can, I hire other people for the things I am not good at.

It speeds up my results and means I am more likely to keep moving forward.

What was the answer to the question I asked you?

What or who could support me to achieve this quicker, easier and with fewer mistakes or barriers?

Take a step forward now in gaining their support; it might well be the best thing you do.

When it comes to igniting your power, being able to break through those inner barriers of repeating old patterns and stories, disconnection from ourselves and isolation are key things for us to pay attention to and continue to work on. As we continue to grow and step up, new stories and patterns might arise. We are always a work in progress, so our work on ourselves is never complete.

Alongside that work, there are three more steps.

Firstly, being TRULY honest with yourself about what you REALLY want. You might be reading this and thinking, "Of course I am honest about what I want."

The reality for many of us is that we diminish what we want or dress it up so it feels better for those around us. Every time we do that, we are not being honest with ourselves or others about the things we want.

I invite you now to sit with yourself in silence, connect with your whole self, and ask yourself these questions:

What is something new I would like to create in my life?

What do I need to let go of to create that?

What new perspective can I have about myself and my ability to create for myself?

Then journal what comes up for you. Don't worry about how you might achieve whatever it is. Don't solutionise straight away. Just sit with the things that you truly desire.

Sometimes, there is resistance to the goals we set because they are not really what we want. Our head tells us the obvious; we settle on that, and then get into action.

That's why it's so important to listen to our gut. Obvious isn't always right.

I am curious to know, if what you were looking to create or achieve at the beginning of this book is still the same now?

When we know what we really want, we need to think about who we need to become for that to happen. Jumping straight into action is often another reason why things don't go to plan.

The step that follows knowing what we really want is forgiveness. It is important to let go of anything that is keeping you stuck: anything you are holding onto that is unhelpful, anything knocking about that is toxic! Take a minute and double-check that you have really let go of anything that will hinder your progress. If there is more to do, grab a scrap of paper and go for it.

The final step of this process is gratitude. When we have an attitude of gratitude, our life is already abundant.

What we appreciate appreciates.

Take a few minutes with your journal and write down everything and everyone you are grateful for in your life. All the experiences and opportunities you have had and still have before you.

Gratitude trumps all other emotions. When we really feel grateful, it is very difficult to feel lack, anxiety, or sadness.

I encourage you to have a daily gratitude practice. You can either journal or do it in your head; whatever works best for you. I do a combination now, but every morning when I was standing on a platform waiting for my train I would think of ten things I was grateful for every day. It helped set my day up in a positive way.

SUMMARY POINTS FOR CHAPTER 5

- Mindset shift: when it comes to you and your life, you are the expert
- There are three main ways even the most successful women block their power: shame, lack and isolation
- We all have stuck energy in our body. This needs to be released so we can bring our whole self to the things we do. This stuck energy can also block our ability to tune into our intuition
- We are not always really honest with ourselves or others about what we really want
- Forgiveness puts us back in control
- Feelings of gratitude trump all other feelings

SPACE FOR YOUR OWN THOUGHTS

SPACE FOR YOUR OWN THOUGHTS

SPACE FOR YOUR OWN THOUGHTS

SPACE FOR YOUR OWN THOUGHTS

CHAPTER 6

THRIVE

THRIVE IN ALIGNMENT

Here we are at the final part of the blueprint. Even when knowing all of the things I have shared in this book and applying all of the tools and techniques, sometimes we fall off track or out of alignment with where we are going and who we need to become.

Alignment helps to keep me and my clients moving forward with our goals.

Remember I mentioned earlier that often we jump straight into action when we set goals for ourselves, yet what we need to do first is think about who we need to be in the realisation of our goals.

Here are my five steps to alignment. I have these typed up on my desk, so I can always remind myself of who I am and where I am going. Get yourself a blank piece of paper, or use your journal, and start completing each step. Then keep this somewhere where you will be reminded of who you are, and each element of alignment, every day.

Step 1 – Commit to who you are becoming. This needs to be an "I am" statement which is growth oriented. It needs to be inspiring and compelling for those times that feel really challenging.

Imagine that you have an important presentation to deliver, but you have disconnected from your brilliance because you are panicking. You are doubting yourself and telling yourself you can't do this, that you are not smart enough, or good enough, or whatever you tell yourself in these moments.

There is no point having an "I am" statement that says, "I can do anything. I am more than enough." You won't believe it. It needs to be something like "I am committed to finding solutions. I am resourceful, curious, and inspired by where I am going".

When you read things like that about yourself, you can shift into curiosity, and start asking yourself "how" which is far more generative and expansive. Committing to a solution is the first stage of a growth mindset, the second is to get curious. Have a think about a growth oriented "I am" statement that is going to keep you moving forward and aligned with your goals, even at the most challenging times.

Step 2 – Let go of unhelpful patterns, stories, and behaviours. For you to step into something new, you need to let go of some baggage. We all have baggage that we need to release.

What are a couple of things that you are leaving behind now? Is it some of your self-talk? Is it procrastination? Is it a belief about yourself?

For me I have learned to let go of my ego and my fear of judgement and failure. This has been so important to me as an entrepreneur because, otherwise, I would get nothing done and be hiding.

What thoughts, habits or behaviours are hindering your success? It's time to release these. Hopefully, you have already identified some of those things to get to this point in the book.

Step 3 – Success is an inside job. We need to create from the inside out, not the outside in! What are two or three things that you will do for yourself, every day, that make you feel good and keep you at your best? For me, it's meditation, walking, journalling (which also helps when I am stuck) and gratitude.

What will you do to help you feel at your best?

Step 4 – Strengths to leverage and growth edges. When it comes to the thing you are looking to create or achieve, what are the three strengths that you can leverage to get you there? Knowing what we are good at and standing confidently in those strengths builds the trust in ourselves we need. Being able to articulate our brilliance confidently helps us be seen for who we really are.

It is equally important to know what we need to work on for us to achieve our goal. I know I am a powerful coach. I know

I have a great head for business and will create opportunities. I know I have the tenacity to see things through. I also know I need help with sales and marketing.

For my success to match my potential, I need to leverage those strengths and work on or hire help for my growth edges.

Take a moment and get really clear now on your three biggest strengths that are critical to your success and your areas of growth, and what you will do about it.

Remember, there is zero shame in growth areas, we all have them. Your power is in seeing them clearly and, if they are necessary for your success, doing something about them.

Step 5 – You might need support around your growth areas. Also, consider the support that will speed up your progress, or make the journey easier and less stressful, with fewer bumps.

There are three types of support that we as humans need:

Emotional support – Who can you go to when you need to share your feelings, without fear of judgement. Whenever we are doing something new, there are going to be moments of doubt, feelings of failure, and all the other stuff that can send us on an emotional rollercoaster. Who are your people? Not the people who make you feel worse than before you spoke to them. The people who make you feel heard and related to, and help you feel lighter after a conversation.

Practical support – Who can you go to when something happens, and you need childcare or animal care support?

What is your contingency plan? What about when you are overloaded at work, and you need support with things at home?

Who is your practical support at work or in your business? Who can you go to when you need help figuring something out, or making something work? If you are new in a role, who is your buddy? Someone that you can ask what feels like the silly questions, without feeling silly.

Professional support – How do you need to grow in your current role or step into your next role? Can you access a coach, mentor, or sponsor through work? It is always a smart move to build your professional network outside of your current organisation. When our network is solely where we work, it is one of the reasons we stay where we are, even when we are not happy!

When you look at support, you will be able to tell where your gaps are and find ways to fill those gaps with the support that you need.

This process continues to fully support me to stay in alignment with where I am going. I hope it does the same for you too.

Who helps you be the best version of you in your career or business? Who can you go to when you want to step up, scale or grow? Who is further ahead and where you want to be that you can learn from?

Pop some names and resources by each type of support (emotional, practical, and professional). Look at where your gaps are, and, if you can, fill them.

Please do look at this every day. When you feel like you are drifting or are out of alignment, it will help you pinpoint where you need to focus.

This is much better than beating yourself up or continuing to go off track.

This is what will enable you to thrive, even when things are tough.

SUMMARY POINTS CHAPTER 6

- Mindset shift: from **what** we are doing to **who** we are becoming
- We all fall out of alignment with where we want to go
- Remembering who we are and where we are going keeps us moving forward
- Check in with the steps every day to make sure you are staying in alignment

SPACE FOR YOUR OWN THOUGHTS

SPACE FOR YOUR OWN THOUGHTS

SPACE FOR YOUR OWN THOUGHTS

SPACE FOR YOUR OWN THOUGHTS

EPILOGUE

In conclusion, I would love for you to remember these things:

- The relationship you have with yourself is the most important relationship you have. Invest in it. Take care of yourself, have compassion for yourself and stay committed to yourself and the things that are important to you.
- When you are outside of your comfort zone, you are growing. In these moments, it is perfectly normal to experience a lack of confidence and self-doubt. These are the moments to focus on the things you can trust in.
- Whatever your goals are, the chances are at times they will feel really difficult and like you are not getting anywhere. These are the moments to dig deep, lean on your support strategies and keep going.
- Learn from and listen to people who have been where you want to go. Take advice from them. Invest in yourself to get where you want to be quicker and more easily, rather than struggling on your own.

Success is not a linear path; there are twists, turns, roadblocks, U-turns and detours. Keep your focus on learning and making progress.

You don't have to do this on your own. Asking for support is a sign of strength.

Use the growth plan and quarterly plan that comes with this book, keep yourself moving forward and appreciate all of your progress.

When it comes to the things you are looking to create in your life, these are the essential ingredients:

- An expansive mindset
- Empowering beliefs
- The skills and capacities necessary to get you there
- Clarity of the first few steps and the destination
- The right support

This book is designed to guide you through each of these elements. In my coaching programme, we delve deeply to help you achieve the transformation you seek.

Now that you have this blueprint, use it to check in on your SPIRIT whenever your confidence wavers. Identify which part of you needs attention and you will know exactly what to do to nurture yourself.

If you haven't already, you might like to take my Unshakeable Confidence Quiz here: https://kirsteen-kldndktp.scoreapp.com/p/main-landing-page

Please believe in your ability to achieve greatness. Your potential is limitless, and every step you take brings you closer to your dreams.

Now you can go forward with unshakeable confidence, knowing that you have the tools, the support, and the resources, internally and externally, to create the life you envision. Your journey is unique, and when you set yourself up for it, your success is inevitable.

If you have any questions or would like to explore these concepts further, please do get in touch with me at kirsteen@elevate-women.co.uk.

SPACE FOR YOUR OWN THOUGHTS

SPACE FOR YOUR OWN THOUGHTS

SPACE FOR YOUR OWN THOUGHTS

SPACE FOR YOUR OWN THOUGHTS

RESOURCES SECTION

The following resources can be found at:

elevate-women.co.uk/unshakeable-confidence-resources-section/

The password is *Unshakeable*

- Check-in audio
- Wheel of life
- Growth and quarterly action plan
- Journaling prompts
- Self-Concept Self-Assessment

HOW YOU CAN WORK WITH ME

I offer one-to-one and group coaching. Check out my website: elevate-women.co.uk

Email Kirsteen@elevate-women.co.uk

Connect with me on LinkedIn: linkedin.com/in/kirsteen-williamson-guinn/

Printed in Dunstable, United Kingdom

63805059R00067